THINK BIG— SHOP SMALL

Unique Stores
and Contemporary
Retail Design

gestalten

New Shores and Opportunities Beckon

Personality is an art honed to perfection by good business
and a focus on the future, across the globe.

You can't change the direction of the wind, but you can set the sails accordingly. Around the planet, successful stores are responding to new challenges with fresh ideas and interiors. The world is changing, and so is retail.

THINK BIG—SHOP SMALL takes you on a journey through exceptional stores, boutiques, and their founders, who are setting their course for the future. The stores and stories on the following pages will surprise you with imaginative designs, fresh aesthetics, and futuristic solutions, along with a deep commitment to their communities.

In New York, for example, sports equipment brand Bala (p. 100) has designed its store as a pastel playground where popular influencers offer regular fitness and meditation classes. In Mykonos, customers at the Greek jewelry store Gavello nel blu (p. 92) can dive deep into an enchanting world of handmade necklaces, rings, and bangles showcased in a blue-tiled poolside setting.

Retailtainment is the name of the concept whereby stores extend their range given to products to include entertainment of many different kinds. Today, exciting designs, brand-compatible events, and a high experiential factor turn these stores into a destination in their own right, drawing customers in and connecting product ranges with positive emotions and memories. Stores themselves are becoming the entertainers, and the retail spaces they occupy are the stages, theme parks, and venues where curated events encourage people to come together. The post-pandemic demand for interactive, in-person experiences remains high. It is indeed telling that some of the stores shown here opened during the COVID-19 lockdowns and are still thriving as of this book's publication.

Technology such as augmented reality, the option to buy online and pick up in-store, and contemporary digital channels offer undreamt-of opportunities. Personalized shopping experiences and seamless service across multiple channels sustain loyalty among customers, who are now much more challenging to retain despite being easier to reach than before the rise of e-commerce. Customers now require consistent and collaborative brand experiences, convenience, entertainment, personal interaction, good advice, and unique products. Major brands such as Apple, Chanel, and Lululemon

"Exciting designs, events and a high experiential factor make stores a destination in their own right."

NEW SHORES AND OPPORTUNITIES BECKON

The straight lines of Axel Arigato (p. 4) and Gavello nel blu (p. 5) and the curves of Altelier (left) and Banema Studio (above) show how architects are rethinking retail design and creating experiential spaces with added emotional value.

are good examples of how powerful and lucrative brand identification can be. Their stores stand out as memorable, unmistakable brand worlds and are seen as such by their target audience. Sales figures have repeatedly proved that the concept of strong brand identification as a driving force is valid. And yet the ubiquitous availability of products online has led to a reversal of the situation. Today, the customer dictates what, where, when, and how purchases are made. Retailers are having to blend culture with commerce and respond to evolving consumer demands in eye-catching ways.

For instance, Milan's boutique Volgare (p. 168) has responded to the challenge with mixed design, strikingly showcasing its men's fashions against an award-winning backdrop of terrazzo, glass, and motorcycle helmets. Altelier (p. 222) in Granada proves that high-end interior design can also work for oil, cured ham, and bread with its gallery-like design that presents delicacies like works of art. Meanwhile, in Tokyo, cosmetics label Officine Universelle Buly (p. 162) has opted for a stunning, double-edged look combining both its history and the future.

The stores chosen for inclusion in THINK BIG—SHOP SMALL represent bold, creative, and inspirational stores from around the world. They have caught the fresh wind of opportunity in their sails and are daring to set out for new shores. Come and discover a store dedicated to preserving the priceless traditions of Argentine artisans; or a specialty store which, thanks to its expertise, is a valued UNESCO partner. Drop anchor in front of a Balinese surf store that has created a small paradise for its neighborhood, then set sail for a Barcelona boutique that welcomes its young customers to a tactile metaverse. We adore design, yearn to discover, and have boundless optimism for the future.

Marianne Julia Strauss is a travel journalist who enjoys writing about the best things in life. Like her debut DO YOU READ ME?, also published by gestalten, THINK BIG—SHOP SMALL celebrates the courage, ingenuity, and magic of the stores that bring our neighborhoods to life.

Here is retailtainment at its purest: Bala's miniature sports world (below) plays with surprising proportions, colors, and shapes. Luph (right) also defies expectations by making solid concrete elements seem lighter than air and as delicate as fine crystal.

ATELIER SUKHA

Fashion
Amsterdam,
Netherlands
Opened in 2011

When Irene Mertens founded her label in 2011, she chose the perfect name in Sanskrit: "Sukha" means "joy" or "well-being." Her Amsterdam store sells sustainable clothing and household accessories made from 100 % natural materials such as wool, linen, cotton, clay, daphne, and cashmere. All the items Suhka sells are locally designed or produced and are carefully selected by Irene.

Atelier Sukha's aesthetic is natural, understated, and timeless. Soft, muted shades dominate the collection and interior, with colorful details adding modern accents. Irene is happy to tell her curious customers why she has fallen in love with particular products in the range. She tells them about the enthusiasm of the manufacturers, explains the sustainability guidelines of the production process, and provides facts about the materials used. Thought-provoking conversations often develop into relationships that are more than just commercial. The love of beautiful, natural materials and environmental protection creates a bond.

If you're into an eco-conscious, mindful lifestyle, you'll love Atelier Sukha. The store is committed to nurturing simplicity, slowing down, and the beauty of small things. Whether it's clothing or bags, porcelain or cleaning spray—this is where you can shop with a clear conscience and support fairly paid partners in Nepal with almost every purchase.

Irene Mertens curates her range in line with her deeply
held convictions. Since Atelier Sukha opened, the
all-important question for her has always been: is the
product good for the planet and the soul?

FACON

Local artisanal objects
Buenos Aires, Argentina
Opened in 2016

Martín Bustamante has traveled well over 70,000 kilometers (40,000 miles) around Argentina since opening Facon. His quest for indigenous crafts, creative design, and ancient traditions regularly takes him to the country's most remote and inaccessible corners. His collected finds, on display in his Buenos Aires boutique, bear witness to Argentina's cultural richness. Hanging next to high-quality, hand-woven rugs are gaucho knives made of carbon steel, backpacks made of leather and sailcloth, and purses made of chaguar—a plant fiber that grows near the Iguazú waterfalls. Every purchase at Facon also supports rural communities. Martín works with NGOs such as Las Warmi, a group of Andean women who weave gorgeous blankets, ponchos, and scarves. He and his business partners are allies with the same worthy goal: preserving Argentine traditions. Facon sees itself as a stage for local artists and artisans, with a collection of stories and a travel guide—in itself a work of art reflecting Argentina's soul.

"Esta casa está abierta para los buenos amigos," reads the sign on the right: "This house is open to good friends." It's the perfect statement from the owner, Martín Bustamante, who describes himself as a passionate host. His store is like a distillery, bringing together the finest treasures from Argentina's 2.8 million square kilometers (1.1 million square miles) in a compact space.

FACON

CARNADA VIVA X FACON

ESTA CASA
ESTA ABIERTA
PARA LOS
BUENOS AMIGOS

SADDLER & CO.

Leather goods
Dubbo, Australia
Opened in 2010

The world seems to spin a little slower at Saddler & Co. When you open the door to this lovingly converted former warehouse, you are knocked back by the smell of wood, genuine leather, and freshly picked foliage. Brass lamps illuminate the store, and the sanded-down wooden floor has been newly whitened. An original wool table, traditionally used in Australian sheep-shearing sheds, serves as the store's tactile centerpiece. Here customers can touch the goods on display.

Since Bede and Jemima Aldridge founded their brand in 2010, the team has grown to include numerous leather workers and artisans from New South Wales. The hallmarks of Saddler & Co.'s high-quality leather goods are durability, regionality, and a deep connection to traditional craftsmanship. Their sleek designs are timeless, elegantly allowing the distinctive nature of the leather hides to shine. Additionally, the store offers customers a leather repair and restoration service, thus fulfilling its promise of being truly sustainable twice over.

One of the many unique features of Saddler & Co. is its workshop—which is directly connected to the store. Through a window, customers can watch the leather goods being made. This builds trust, vividly tells the story of the high-quality craft, and provides an exciting insight into an art form that is now rare, flourishing in just a few places, but all the more beautiful for it.

STUDIO AUGUSTINE

Concept store
Marrakech, Morocco
Opened in 2023

Tiny Studio Augustine is hidden behind an inconspicuous entrance. Dutch interior designer and hotelier Willem Smit has opened the third part of his celebrated House of Augustine collection with this store. So far, the collection includes a villa in Tangier and a riad in Marrakech. Studio Augustine is his way of inviting shoppers to embrace shopping as a conscious experience.

Customers can browse the range of Moroccan furniture and handicrafts, fragrances, and clothing at their leisure. The collection includes a caftan designed by Willem, books, and vintage finds. Customers can have their favorite items delivered to their homes within four to six weeks. The walls, currently a warm saffron yellow, change color depending on the collection. Up to ten times a year, Studio Augustine also hosts its exclusive First Thursday for small groups of no more than ten invited guests, who enjoy private cultural events such as readings, film screenings, dinners with live cooking, or exhibitions.

Studio Augustine celebrates Moroccan craftsmanship from its floor—lined with glazed herringbone tiles from Fez—to its ceiling. With a traditional yet eclectic selection, the store successfully captures the vibrant vibe of contemporary Marrakech. Its fresh interpretations of traditional styles and exciting interior details are an inspiration in themselves. Come and have a browse!

Dinner essentials
New York, New York, USA
Opened in 2021

What could be more inviting than a lovingly laid table full of delicacies? To answer that question, Katherine Lewin has whipped up a dazzling store that stocks everything you might need to host a successful dinner party. Big Night's shelves and refrigerators are stocked with olives, crackers, and deli items ranging from dips to chili oil, all of which are most beautifully served in ceramic bowls, plates, and dishes that are also for sale. In addition, the former food editor also sells pretty glasses, cutlery sets, candles, linen napkins, and select table decorations from around the world. Katherine intentionally sources over half of the fine foods on offer from women-owned businesses.

Erica Padgett of Decorum Design Build in New York City designed the store to make visitors feel like they are guests at a particularly stylish friend's house—one who's happy to offer tips for dinner parties and make every customer feel confident that every night can be a Big Night.

The COVID-19 pandemic put a long pause on dinner parties. Once it felt safer to gather with friends, Katherine Lewin took matters into her own hands, and in less than three months, she opened Big Night. Her selection of cheeses, charcuterie, snacks, sauces, and sweets—plus everything you might want to serve them—is a one-stop shop for hosting.

KAKIMORI

Stationery
Tokyo, Japan
Opened in 2010

Takuma Hirose has created a little paradise stemming from the Japanese love of writing. Kakimori produces made-to-order notebooks, with customers choosing the covers and paper from a carefully curated selection. In the central workspace, customers are welcome to watch the notebooks being crafted. The popular stationery store also sells handmade items by Japanese artisans, as well as fine paper, fountain pens, and designer pencils from around the world.

Kakimori is located in one of Tokyo's historic Shitamachi districts, where workshops and retail shops remain an integral part of a tight-knit community. Customers are friends here and vice versa. As if symbolically, the wood and colored stripes of the interior's herringbone pattern are interwoven throughout the store, creating a harmonious whole. Shogo Kawata of the Japanese firm teamLab Architects also designed the upper floor of Kakimori, where customers can mix their own ink in front of a wall of gradations ranging from the lightest azure to dark thunderstorm blue.

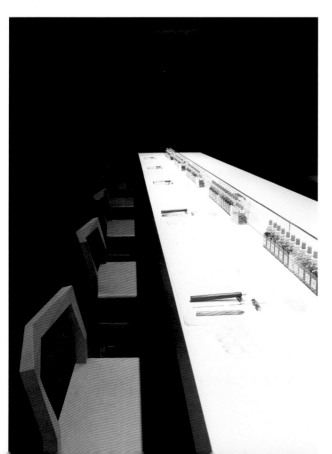

Favorite Colors: Local, Vibrant, Diverse

A well-known German saying asks the question "Why search so far afield when good things are so near?"

Still Here is the name of a denim store in New York, proclaiming an ambition that all independent stores surely aspire to. Every purchase at Still Here supports local, sustainable production, secures jobs, and maintains an element of diversity that is as desirable and worth defending in the retail sector as anywhere else.

We know that healthy societies thrive on a diversity of ideas, like healthy bodies thrive on a varied diet. At the same time, nature is at its healthiest when it is at its most vibrant. In life, diversity is not simply a nice add-on—it is a prerequisite.

The natural world of commerce is not so different. While large chains resemble monocultures, local stores like Still Here are like carefully tended gardens with a diverse range of local species and even rare plants that benefit us all—culturally and commercially.

In the 1990s, anyone strolling through the pedestrian shopping area of a typical small town could browse in a colorful hardware store, press their nose against the window of the local pet store, discuss the latest vinyl at the record store, and get advice from the knowledgeable owners of the local bookstore. Buzzing and humming on every corner, small towns teemed with life.

Today, huge home improvement stores, pet store chains, and online commerce have sucked the life out of many independent stores. Once-distinctive pedestrian zones, with their often idiosyncratic stores (and store owners) that attracted customers from surrounding towns, have become virtually interchangeable.

Bookstores are an excellent example of local, independent commerce still going strong. Those that have survived never rested on their laurels.

Instead, they have kept up with the times, cultivating social media channels and running well-organized online stores. Moreover, they organize regular events, network with neighborhoods and schools, deliver the latest books to older customers in person, and prioritize local literature and local travel guides.

As a result, the most successful bookstores have established themselves as an essential mainstay of urban communities and leverage several unique selling points that set them apart from large chains and online retailers. Their colorful gardens

"In life, diversity is not simply a nice 'add-on'—it is a prerequisite. The natural world of commerce is not so different."

Local in spite of global: Marin Montagut (p. 36) only sells treasures made in France. Originario (left) in Mexico City and Alara (above) in Lagos, Nigeria, show us what modern love of your homeland can look like.

have borne the fruit of friendship and a sense of community, and the stores are deeply rooted in a genuine sense of local identity.

Local color has a lot to do with identity. What local, independent stores contribute with passion and purpose are, by definition, absent from the less natural world of large, international chains whose stores around the planet sell the exact same range of products, primarily irrespective of local context. This global, one-size-fits-all principle may be lucrative and frequently practical for some; however, it means that people from Japan to Greenland tend to be stuck following the same fashion trends or

create the same interiors. Yet, surely, identity is ultimately the answer to the age-old question of "Who am I?" and satisfies a basic human need to strike the right balance between a sense of individuality and a sense of belonging.

Local businesses have a unique opportunity to address this deep-seated desire while upholding traditions that are worth protecting. In Buenos Aires, Facon (p. 16) sells original handicrafts from all over Argentina. Through its collaborations, the store supports remote communities and sustains local customs while benefiting from their distinctive selection. Originario in Mexico City operates on the same principle. The store offers local artists a stage and enriches its neighborhood with a constant stream of new ideas. In Lebanon, Images d'Orient (p. 210) focuses on local specialties. The owners source their exceptional ceramics, vases, and accessories exclusively from Lebanese artists, thus actively protecting a piece of national cultural heritage.

Local stores supporting local arts, crafts, and traditions—is that the winning formula? Local all the way? Many of the stores featuring in THINK BIG—SHOP SMALL flourish in places that are not as profitable for large monocultures to cultivate, and these small gardens thrive all the better for it. In New York, Still Here seems to have found one of those sweet spots. Their bestselling jeans with a characteristic vertical stripe are just one of a thousand splashes of local color in the neighborhood. It's a manifesto well-suited to local identity, cultural diversity, and a future where our towns and cities can bloom like beautiful, colorful, and healthy gardens. Perhaps it's time to rebrand the denim store as "Here To Stay."

Studio Augustine (below) in Marrakech represents local artisans from all over Morocco, thereby maintaining cherished local traditions. TAP (right) is a concept store that has become a hub for independent practitioners from all over Vietnam and operates on a similar basis.

FAVORITE COLORS: LOCAL, VIBRANT, DIVERSE

MERCHANT

Interiors
Los Angeles,
California, USA
Opened in 2014

Who hasn't dreamed of bringing that Moroccan rug or mid-century dresser from their vacation home to their own living room? Artist Denise Portmans and her daughter Sara Marlowe Hall have turned that idea into a beautiful reality. If you drive east from Los Angeles and turn left just before Joshua Tree National Park, you'll come to Morongo Valley. Here, in the middle of the California desert, is arguably the most inviting storefront in the state.

Merchant House High Desert is a vacation home you can book—with a difference. Items similar to the furnishings and accessories in the home are on sale in the label's stores. Mother and daughter share their love of art, design, and warm interiors in the lovingly furnished Merchant House. Customers, or rather guests, are only too happy to be inspired here by the cushions, art, and curiosities on display. And anyone who buys their favorite piece at Merchant in West or East Los Angeles will take home a part of their desert vacation.

In its Los Angeles store, Merchant offers its customers a choice of a thousand treasures, large and small. Here, in addition to the beautiful array of products, customers can benefit from expert advice and invaluable interior design tips.

The vacation home Merchant House High Desert shows how homey the
furniture and art objects from the store can look in a domestic setting. For
$450 a night, up to four guests can relax in this harmonious dream space.

HENNE

Fashion
Melbourne, Australia
Opened in 2022

For the first boutique for Henne, their fashion label, Nadia Bartel, Michelle Ring, and Laura Broque chose two separate, adjoining retail stores. In order to convey the warm character of the much-loved online store in the corresponding interior, the three co-founders consulted interdisciplinary designer Brahman Perera. His multi-sensory design is characterized by natural colors, striking visuals, and a variety of textures ranging from velvety soft to rough.

In the store's "Her Space" area, art and literature provide a sophisticated backdrop to the latest collections. Hand-knotted wool rugs contrast with the sleek aluminum counter, which has been hand-treated with wax. The upstairs dressing rooms have been crafted from woven seaweed. The second area, the "Atelier," is used for events, workshops, dressmaking, and fittings. Here, customers are offered personal advice and invited to get creative and look behind the scenes of the label—an experience in complete contrast to shopping online.

The designers have paired sleek pipe installations and theatrical mirrors using rich caramel tones and wool white. Books and art give the fashion store a home-like feel.

In the studio, hand-woven kilims and textured walls create
a cozy atmosphere. Customers can participate in workshops
and get style advice in this private setting.

FRAMA STUDIO STORE

Lifestyle
Copenhagen, Denmark
Opened in 2017

Frama deliberately chose this historic pharmacy in the Nyboder district for their Copenhagen Studio Store. Its original, intricately decorated oak cabinets contrast starkly with the brand's diverse contemporary designs while simultaneously evoking the late 19th century. The designers like to draw inspiration from the history of their showroom. Their designs frequently feature reverential references to past design eras. Frama designs furniture, kitchens and lighting, books, clothing, and fragrances, as well as complete interiors. The common factors are simple forms, natural materials, and an attitude to life that is located somewhere between permanence and modernity.

      With regular events for the creative scene, the Studio Store provides another welcome offering. Since October 2020, the in-house café Apotek 57 has been serving homemade delicacies with—it goes without saying—an emphasis on simplicity, seasonal ingredients, and clean lines.

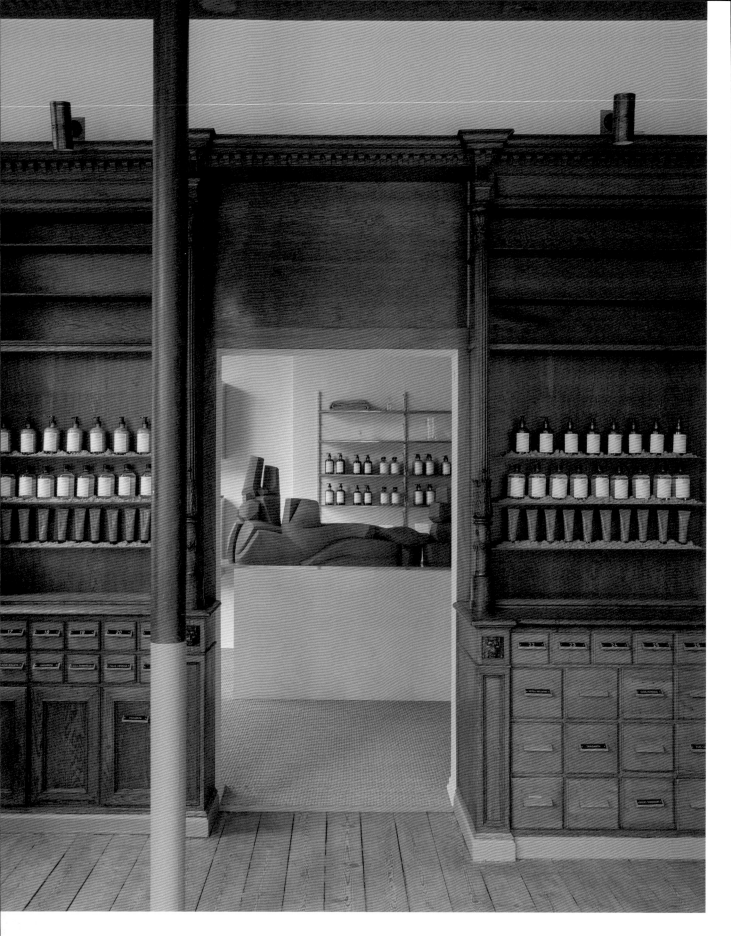

The modern Capsule Shop in the Frama Studio Store is its own little world. The designers' goal was to create a space that seamlessly ties in with the original historic rooms of St. Paul's Apotek. Seagrass, warm earth tones, and wood provide atmospheric continuity. Frama has also created a separate space where you can experience and test its own range of skincare products and fragrances.

TAKIZME

Tea
Tokyo, Japan
Opened in 2021

Since time immemorial, the Japanese tea ceremony has stood for tranquility, con-centration, and presence. Takizme reverentially delivers on that promise, while breaking with tradition. For his modern version of the tea store, Takuya Takizme commissioned Japanese product designer Ryota Yokozeki to create a contemporary interior. Traditionally, the **furo**, the brazier for preparing tea, is made of ceramic or metal. Here, though, the designer created it primarily from light-colored Ōya stone, a heat-resistant tuff stone from Tochigi Prefecture. The shelves for the tea bowls are made of paulownia wood, used to make furniture in Japan since ancient times because of its lightness and high level of moisture control. In between the wood, copper adds shimmering accents. The table also represents a modern inter-pretation of the national design philosophy. Made using the traditional method of **sashimono**, without nails, it folds elegantly and, when assembled, forms a T and a Z, symbolizing the name Takizme.

Tea has been attributed with miraculous powers since time immemorial. Its traditional infusion brings people together, lifts spirits, and at the same time, warms hands and hearts. Takizme strives to pass on this heritage. Its contemporary tea offering is rooted in Japanese history and is aimed at modern customers who need to recharge their batteries and harmonize mind, body, and soul.

HIGASHIYA GINZA

Traditional Japanese candy
Tokyo, Japan
Opened in 2009

When Higashiya Ginza starts selling its delicious, pink, flower-shaped **wagashi**, it's a sign that spring is on its way. An elevator ride takes you worlds away from the hustle and bustle of the surrounding shopping district and into this famous candy store in Pola Center, two floors above street level. Here, in October 2009, Shinichiro Ogata opened this little oasis for food lovers. Natural materials such as wood and copper blend harmoniously, following the principles of yin and yang, and provide the setting for the freshly prepared **wagashi**. The Japanese confections are well-known for creatively reflecting the seasons in their flavors and designs.

Shinichiro Ogata is constantly developing new, reverential reinterpretations of centuries-old traditional recipes, which he sells in packaging he has also designed. The best place to enjoy the delicious daifuku, mochi, and other treats is the tea salon of the Higashiya Ginza—before returning to the streets of Tokyo freshly fortified and enriched with many sweet memories.

Higashiya Ginza's in-house tea salon (top left) sees itself as a modern interpretation of traditional Japanese sabō, or tea house. Up to 40 patrons can enjoy modern tea ceremonies here, relaxing in the curved wooden armchairs around the stone tea counter at the heart of the salon.

CHENJINGKAIOFFICE

Made-to-measure shoes
Taipei, Taiwan
Opened in 2008

Minimalist, customized, and versatile: chenjingkaioffice's interior and product range share the same attributes. In this simple Taipei store, the team led by designer Chen Jing-Kai produces fine, made-to-measure shoes ranging from sneakers to elegant men's dress shoes. The friendly sales team provides on-site advice and helps you select the right leather, soles, eyelets, and laces. Naturally, life-long maintenance service for the shoes is included in the price.

Chen Jing-Kai opened his office in 2008 as a design studio, and since then it has organically evolved into the store it is today. However, the designer sees his made-to-measure shoes as just part of a more comprehensive overall concept. In addition to its function as a studio and sales space, chenjingkaioffice currently serves as a venue for exhibitions and creative events. In the future, the store will become an experimental platform, bringing together artisans, suppliers, retailers, and customers as variable components of artistic collaborations—a perfect fit!

134

chenjingkaioffice®

Customers Forming Communities

To foster their local communities, stores are expanding their offerings to include game nights, skate parks, and student cafés.

How fitting that commerce and community both start with "comm." Around the world, more and more stores are wowing their customers with a genuine commitment to building strong communities. Independent retailers host custom events and educational workshops; offer attractive places to hang out, learn, and celebrate; or invite customers to linger in their in-house cafés, indoor playgrounds, or art spaces—thus making their mark where online commerce simply can't.

It's unmistakable that physical stores are more essential than ever for cultivating authentic customer relationships. Two years of a pandemic are certainly no counterpart for over two million years of human evolution.

Our requirement for companionship is even more deeply rooted than our desire for the latest scented hand cream or wine-red designer chairs. But at the same time, retailers of all sizes are having to adapt their customer recruitment methods to new realities. Life has become more hybrid. More and more people are working from home, and anywhere else on the planet you can think of. At the click of a button, products of all kinds can be delivered right to your doorstep within days or even hours. Social media and advertising are merging in a cacophony of influencers and key words. You can only win if you think innovatively and radically and look ahead.

The Drifter surf store in Uluwatu, Bali, takes a particularly inclusive approach. The owners have created an entire surfing microcosm here. In addition to surfboards, shorts, and accessories, the store also sells books and local art related to surfing. Then, adjacent to the sales area, there is the in-house café-restaurant, which serves healthy smoothies and is also popular with both tourists and locals as a co-working space. Anyone looking for surfing lessons can access the local network of operators here, and in this way, also support the Balinese community.

Avenue&Son (p. 112) in Shanghai follows the same philosophy, but for the skateboarding community. The skateboard label added a phenomenal marble skate park to its flagship store, and it quickly became a hotspot for the neighborhood. Between flips and grinds, in view of a stunning skyline, skaters can chill at the integrated kiosk.

"Today, authentic communities and genuine personal interaction are taking successful stores to the next level."

Whether it's cannabis or tea you're after, Superette Annex (p. 70) and Kettl Tea (p. 71) embrace the idea of enjoyment with friends. At Pansy (left), customers gather for craft events. The surf store Drifter (above), brings locals and tourists together.

On the other side of the world, in Brooklyn, local tea afficionados can meet for tea classes, tastings, and game nights regularly hosted by the small, independent tea store Kettl Tea. The community principle is also catching on increasingly in Milan. The Italian hand care label Permano (p. 104) invites people to community wellness events and workshops in its mint-green store Spazio Permano.

Today, authentic communities, genuine personal interaction, and creative togetherness are taking successful stores to the next level. For brick-and-mortar retailers, the opportunity to meet up IRL, i.e., "in real life," represents the most important unique selling point over online retailing. Its advantages radiate life in color and in three dimensions. To this end, stores are becoming multifaceted, deliberately positioning themselves broadly, cooperating with delivery services, getting involved in schools, serving up little delicacies, supporting local sports clubs, and offering their product ranges in their own online stores. As Aristotle knew: "The whole is greater than the sum of its parts."

In Amsterdam, Pansy shows us how it's done. The creative store sells cute, unique items to give as gifts or to keep for yourself. In addition, customers can design, glaze, and fire their own ceramics in the store's in-house workshop. With the help of independent artists, you can create your own cups and teapots and make new friends.

Superette (p.198) also relies on friendship. This small chain for cannabis products has deliberately opened one of its stores in close proximity to the local college, and it has quickly become a popular social space for students. You can smoke and munch by the high boards (pun intended) while you learn and philosophize.

Although it's surfboards, ceramics or tea, the community is at the top of the "to-support" list of modern stores—not least thanks to competition from the web, which is effectively forcing retailers to become better, more versatile versions of themselves. No pressure, no diamonds!

Where previously there was little call for it, today, every store can—with imagination, budget, and commitment—become a place that brings people and neighborhoods together and thus provides added emotional value and support. Every store can become an institution that, in addition to commerce and community, adds commitment to its sign. And it is those stores that will become favorites, underscoring one of the core mantras of marketing: People shop with their hearts.

The Sorgenfri community (below) is supported by a committed artist collective and enjoys meeting in the store's own coffee shop. Avenue&Son (right) supports the skateboarding community with curbs, rails, and sponsorship.

THE MAKER STORE

Arts & crafts
Amsterdam, Netherlands
Opened in 2016

When De Hallen was renovated under the direction of Dutch architect André van Stigt, the Amsterdam municipality made sustainable use a condition. Thus, its prior use by an artists' collective had to be carried on. In 2016, Victor van Doorn and Siem Meijerink won the bid with their imaginative concept, which had deep local roots, and they moved into the old streetcar depot along with a handful of other independent stores.

The Maker Store represents over 80 artists and craftspeople ("makers"), all of whom are local to Amsterdam. The team maintains personal connections with the makers and knows the faces and stories behind each brand. Meanwhile, the makers here have direct contact with their customers. At the monthly Maker Market, which takes place right outside the store, other small brands also showcase their products and network with vendors from all over the Netherlands. Creativity, a genuine sense of community, and an overriding passion for craftsmanship unite them and their Amsterdam colleagues.

OLD SOULS

Outdoor
Cold Spring,
New York, USA
Opened in 2013

When Tara and James Caroll found the right space for their outdoor store, Old Souls, they stripped it down to the load-bearing walls and ceiling joists to create their own vision of the perfect store. Removing the old false ceiling gave the store a fantastic ceiling height of 3.7 m (12 ft.), allowing the space to show off solid wood and extensive product selection.

The couple deliberately avoided traditional retail displays, opting instead for a recycled and do-it-yourself approach. The walls are made of a mix of softwoods: pine, fir, and hemlock from an old tobacco warehouse in the South. The Carolls found the oak for the floor in a Pennsylvania cow barn. A mechanic's fan belt display has been modified to display belts instead. The clothing racks were made from raw steel by a local craftsman. The Carolls are avid fly fishers, and they love to advise their growing regular clientele on unforgettable adventures in the great outdoors. They also organize popular fly-fishing trips to destinations from Cuba to Kiribati.

Behind its 19th-century façade, Old Souls looks like a cozy log cabin in the woods. The license plates on the wall come from the many fly-fishing trips that have taken Tara and James Caroll from Iceland to the South Pacific. Although they order their merchandise from around the world, their primary focus is on products made locally and elsewhere in the USA.

BOTÁNICA FLORERÍA

Plants
San Pedro Garza García,
Mexico
Opened in 2013

Mexican florist Vicky Dehesa's aim is to appeal to all the senses in her store Botánica Florería. Your eyes feast on lush greenery and surprising color compositions. Pretty candles smell of sandalwood, vanilla, and more. Soft music plays in the background. Plants with plump leaves invite you to brush against them, and spiky cactus spines warn you to proceed with caution. Vicky likes to offer her customers homemade cocoa, coffee, or nibbles with nut butter as they browse.

Her modern bouquets combine a natural feel with contemporary aesthetics. In addition, Botánica Florería sells attractive accessories such as flower pots, planters, floral souvenirs, and miniature works of art. Still, the décor takes second place to the flourishing range of plants. Upright bricks double as platforms for the plants; glass light fixtures hang from the ceiling on ropes and are reflected in the geometric wall mirrors. The soft green hue of the walls and the abundance of wood underscore the urban jungle flair—or, more accurately, blossoming life.

Embracing a thoroughly aesthetic design, Botánica Florería's owner has been a successful designer herself for many years. Vicky Dehesa always integrates contemporary trends and currents into her personal ideas about pleasing aesthetics. After all, aren't individuality and originality precisely what customers want?

WILD SOULS

Nut butter
Athens, Greece
Opened in 2019

Warning—highly addictive! Behind its bright façade, Wild Souls sells nothing but delicious nut butters. From the e-shop, you can order soft pistachio butter, crunchy peanut butter, or melt-in-the-mouth almond butter with dates and cocoa. Or you can buy them on the spot, in beautiful little jars, or try them immediately with a fresh organic coffee—after all, who wouldn't want to linger here awhile? For the owner, Areti Kyriotou, Wild Souls is a philosophy she wants to share with her customers.

All the nut butters are free of sugar, palm oil, and preservatives, so the natural flavor of the nuts is fully retained. What's more, the store's operations are entirely waste- and plastic-free. Areti designed the vibrant orange interior with Miltos Kontogiannis, creative director at the Greek design studio studiomateriality. Their goal was to create a simple and unique store full of good energy and give the nourishing nuts—or "wild treasures," as the store calls them—a fitting showcase. Mission accomplished!

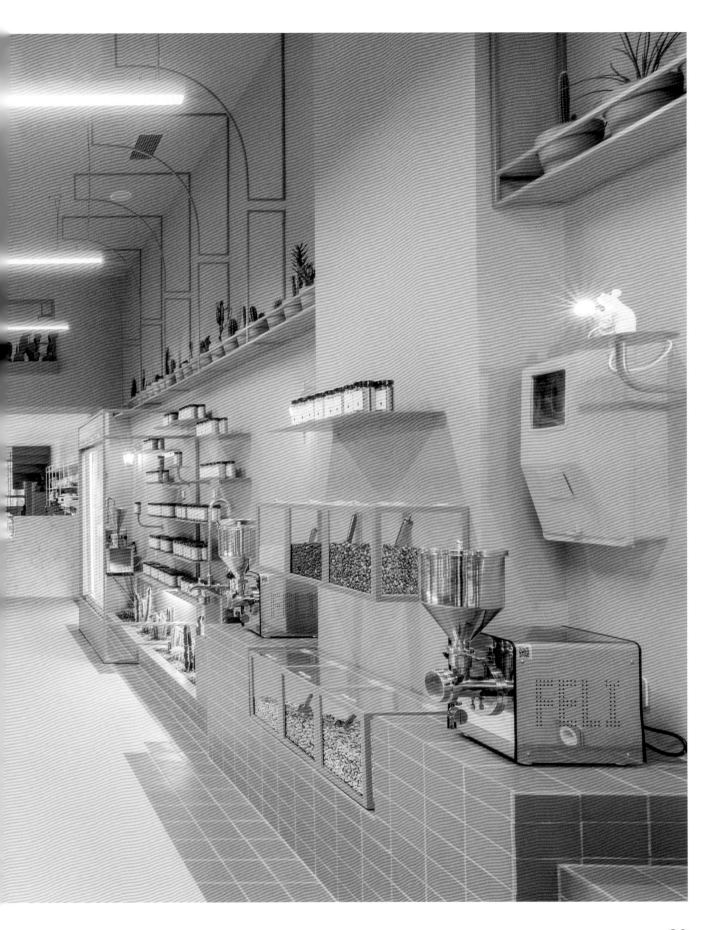

If you're feeling a little wild, a taste of Wild Souls's nut butter is just the ticket.
After all, as Hippocrates once said, "You are what you eat." In this case, however,
you could also put the wild feeling down to the gorgeous interior—bright orange
is known to create energy and a good mood. Case closed. Seconds, please!

GAVELLO NEL BLU

Jewelry
Mykonos, Greece
Opened in 2021

Is it a pool? Well, almost—but instead of water, you'll see Martha and Elizabetta Gavello's timeless jewelry sparkling here. For the store's design, the mother and daughter team and interior design studio Saint of Athens drew inspiration from the aesthetics of cult film director Wes Anderson, the jet-set images of U.S. photographer Slim Aarons, and works by the versatile British artist David Hockney.

The blue tiles covering the walls, floors, and display units in the shop are the work of the Greek team Dive Architects. The simple extravagance perfectly reflects the soul of the Italian label Gavello and contrasts with the traditional Cycladic storefront. Filigree chains shimmer on marbled towel hooks. Beach balls, red and white cushions, and a pool ladder evoke the fashionable bathing paradise of Mykonos, turning the visitor into the protagonist of a playful story. Immerse yourself here, and somewhere between the summer vibes and the surrealism, you might discover a new favorite item.

One of the most heartwarming things about the Gavello label is
that it all began with a love story. Martha Gavello and her husband,
Rinaldo, created their first designs in the late 1970s and continued
to develop their shared vision. It was clear to the couple that every
piece of jewelry merited fine craftsmanship, simple design, and an
underlying meaning.

Gavello's jewelry derives the underlying meaning from spiritual references and powerful symbols. Crosses, all-seeing eyes, and light-refracting gemstones weave through the collections like common threads. Today, their daughter Elisabetta Gavello, is responsible for the design process and brand identity, guiding the company's creative journey.

BALA

Sports equipment
New York, New York, USA
Opened in 2022

Bala knows that life is more beautiful in pastels! Designer Madelynn Ringo envisaged the sports brand's New York flagship store as a sculptural playground. Oversized models of sports accessories conjure up a unique dreamscape where customers love to take selfies for social media posts. A ceiling-high Bala Beam in a delicate hue of sage rests against the wall in a corner, reflected on all sides in the surrounding mirrors. An oversized version of the popular Bala Bangle becomes a cozy, sand-colored seat. With its chromatic design, the store physically transports you into the brand's pastel-colored world.

And if you feel like trying out your recently purchased sports equipment right away, you can do so in the store's fitness and meditation classes. Well-known fitness influencers lead in-house courses such as "Balacize," actively incorporating the interior, providing professional tips for athletes, and cultivating the fitness community—along with new friendships.

This pastel-colored fitness store's simple but effective formula is: (texture + color + scale) × surprise. A three-meter-high (ten-foot-) black model of the famous Power Ring marks the entrance to the flagship store. It stretches from wall to wall, creating a threshold that allows visitors to leave the Soho neighborhood behind and enter the dream world of Bala.

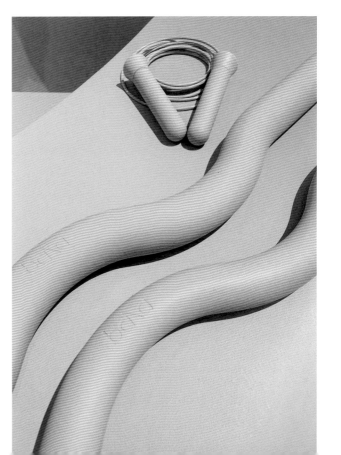

SPAZIO PERMANO

Hand care
Milan, Italy
Opened in 2022

Just one year after Permano's online launch, the Italian hand care label opened a Milan store as clean and sustainable as the brand itself. The interior was designed by untitled architecture in collaboration with Edoardo Giaroli. The focus on a communal shopping experience was Permano's main goal—after the COVID-19 pandemic, it was vital for the store to appeal through its community spirit. When you enter, the first thing that catches your eye is the monolithic table, the centerpiece of the store. Two frames placed on opposite walls reinforce the symmetry of the store, which is painted a muted light green. An infographic mirror visually expands the space. Vertical, minimalist displays showcase the products. They are within easy reach of the table, inviting visitors to explore Permano's skincare offerings together. Collaborative wellness events, hand care treatments, and workshops take place here regularly, as well. In this way, Spazio Permano nurtures its customers' hands and the community experience—literally up close and personal.

The custom-built concrete washbasin (above) illustrates
the experiential nature of Spazio Permano. Here, customers
can try out the hand scrubs and soaps on offer, and more.

BANEMA STUDIO

Design concepts
Lisbon, Portugal
Opened in 2020

The Portuguese architects Campos Costa Arquitetos proposed a radical two-fold solution for Dulce and Manuel Joaquim Neves's extraordinary store. Two large structures divide the store on a single floor. While Banema Lab on the right appears sleek and functional, Banema Studio is dominated by curved lines. The two parts complement each other visually and in terms of content. In Banema Lab, architects, designers, artisans, and private clients can find inspiration on textures and colors, get answers to technical questions, contact experts, and access an almost infinite selection of materials for furniture, home furnishings, and more.

In the Banema Studio, on the other hand, selected objects, fragrances, and decorative accessories from around the world are on sale alongside fine specialty coffees. The company's roots date back to 1964, when its founder began selling wood-based materials. Today, with its contemporary and holistic approach, Banema is passing on this legacy to a new generation of artisans.

If customers cannot get to a company's faraway headquarters, the company has to get to the customer. Banema opened its second branch under this banner. The idea was to bring together design brands from around the world. The result is a dazzling new take on what an interior design, architecture, and building showroom can look like.

AVENUE&SON

Skateboards
Shanghai, China
Opened in 2021

Stephen Khou, Dan Leung, Jeremy Hu, and Boss Xie, quite literally found their fortune on the streets of Shanghai. The four professional skateboarders are like superstars in China, and they fulfilled a dream in 2014 by founding their skateboard brand, Avenue&Son. Various Associates were hired to design the first flagship store. The Chinese design team shadowed skateboarders on their daily rides and strove to decipher the DNA of the most popular skateboarding spots.

What did they find? Halfpipes, common in skate parks, are apparently not a favorite among skateboarders. Instead, skaters prefer stairs, railings, and other everyday features of the cityscape, because the edges make perfect grinds and jumps possible. Armed with this information, the designers developed a premium version of a skate park. Solid marble compactly replicates the most popular skate spots on the street, and skaters can also socialize over drinks at an open-air kiosk. The bronze logo of Avenue&Son was engraved into the stone in accordance with tradition. The skate park also serves as a space for various events that occur here regularly, and it's not just the phenomenal view that makes them so popular.

Popular perceptions of skateboarding have changed ever since it was recognized as an official sport at the 2020 Summer Olympics in Tokyo. What was once a fun street sport has become a serious contender and part of a lucrative industry. Avenue&Son alone sponsor more than 20 professional skaters in China and internationally—and the trend is growing.

MASA

Bread
Bogotá, Colombia
Opened in 2011

It's in the nature of a bakery to quickly become the favorite neighborhood hangout. With its startling architecture and truly delicious bread, Masa is more like a next evolutionary step. Ever since the Colombian sisters Silvana and Mariana Villegas opened their bakery in 2011, it quickly became a fixture on the Bogotá food scene—thanks in no small part to its design.

       Architect Benjamin Cadena, the founder of New York-based Studio Cadena, designed Masa as a composition of different spatial volumes. Behind the cut-out façade, the central entrance opens into the accompanying café and separate retail space. The outdoor terrace provides garden seating and connects the public areas with the bakery at the rear of the building. The long concrete counter, wood-clad service station and communicative seating platform sculpt the space while creating plenty of room for customers. As Masa is well aware: bread tastes best in the company of others.

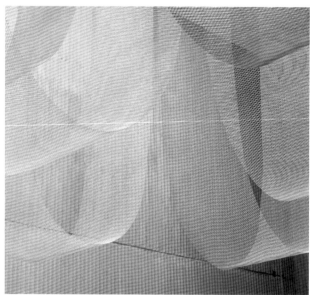

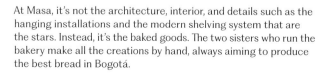

At Masa, it's not the architecture, interior, and details such as the hanging installations and the modern shelving system that are the stars. Instead, it's the baked goods. The two sisters who run the bakery make all the creations by hand, always aiming to produce the best bread in Bogotá.

TAP

Handicrafts
Ho Chi Minh City,
Vietnam
Opened in 2015

Creative arts and crafts label TAP spent four years working on its store concept in Ho Chi Minh City. The team designed the interior in collaboration with the Vietnamese design firm Sawadeesign Studio, which created a translucent, gently floating ambience for the approximately 80 square-meter (860-square-foot) retail space. The challenge, posed by the building's owner: the floors and walls of the historic building could not be altered.

As a solution, the designers opted for unfired tiles laid directly on the floor without glue or leveling compound. Even the lightweight shelves are not fixed but are free-standing. Visitors can glide through the space in a museum-like fashion to reach the small sand garden, where they can relax and become part of the installation themselves. The product range is every bit the equal to the innovative design of the store. In addition to its own products, TAP also showcases other brands from Vietnam, promotes independent manufacturers, and deliberately focuses on healthy growth—like the tree that breaks through TAP's walls and out into the open.

Welcome to the Specialists

Highly specialized stores come closest to perfection when their focus is sharpest.

Anyone looking for one of the most delicious nut butters in the world will sooner or later end up in Athens, in a small side street behind Syntagma Square—in a bright orange store, no less. Here, Wild Souls (p. 86) exclusively sells smooth almond butter, soft pistachio butter, creamy peanut butter, cashew butter to die for, and crunchy hazelnut butter with cocoa and dates. And it's been a huge success since it opened in 2019.

Highly specialized stores are a phenomenon that seems to defy all laws of economics. Yet they work—for a thousand reasons.

For example, Wild Souls's customers not only love the seemingly endless selection of nut butters but also value the owner's expertise, and her enthusiasm for nut butters and fairtrade, all-natural, and environmentally conscious production is evident in every sentence she utters. Here, with every purchase, you also get a piece of her heart and soul. All a bit picture-book, you think? Possibly, but it's real.

Often, specialty stores turn out to be their own little worlds or wonderlands where you can lose yourself completely. Across the continent and the English Channel, the enchanting store Alice Through The Looking Glass (p. 176) sells a variety of carefully curated books, accessories, and ceramics centered around the famous story **Alice in Wonderland**. Enthusiasts from all over the world make pilgrimages to London to admire "not-for-sale" first editions or to treat themselves to white porcelain rabbits or Alice art prints. The store's specialism is so effective that museums worldwide repeatedly request loans from the store.

Even global institutions have been known to request the expertise of specialized stores, for example UNESCO. Deyrolle (p. 144), a historic taxidermy store in Paris, runs an educational vegetable garden in collaboration with UNESCO, thus continuing to carry through its self-proclaimed educational mission.

The extent to which highly specialized stores regard themselves as experts in their fields rather than just normal businesses is something they continue to demonstrate successfully. At a time when the Internet is full of unsolicited and unchecked advice, the demand for in-depth, sound knowledge on specific topics is greater than ever.

"Highly specialized stores are a phenomenon that seems to defy all laws of economics. Yet they work."

In the mood for greens? o'flower (p.122) and Sip 'n' Smoke (p.123), respectively, sell flowers and anything involving cannabis. The sweets from Higashiya Ginza (above) and the nut butters from Wild Souls (left) are absolutely delicious.

In effect, specialty stores are like editors-in-chief, researchers, and guardians of their specialty areas—and their staff's jobs depend on making the right decisions, building bridges between their knowledge and that of their customers, keeping their finger on the pulse, and to some extent, being able to look into the future. After all, where else but in a specialized store can you expect to find the latest information and trends on a particular subject matter?

In New York City, the store Big Night (p.28) stocks just about everything you might need for an unforgettable dinner party, from appetizers and centerpieces to glassware and linens. Owner Katherine Lewin clairvoyantly opened her store at the onset of the pandemic. A former restaurant editor, she is adept at advising her clientele, drawing on a wealth of knowledge, experience, and contacts. Her passion for dinner parties shines more brightly here than any neon sign.

Is it a coincidence that isolation is considered one of the most critical factors for evolution? If a store adopts a particularly focused approach, honing their niche and fostering discussion and exchange of knowledge, undreamt-of growth is virtually inevitable. When the visionary founders of Superette (p.198) decided to open small stores all over Toronto to sell cannabis products, their bold approach was vindicated by immediate success. Branches such as Sip 'n' Smoke (p.202) humorously and harmoniously blend in with the neighborhood and serve not only as a specialty store, but also as a meeting place for like-minded people, and a reliable outlet for specialist goods and information. More establishments are already being planned.

Since these highly specialized stores prioritize quality over quantity, they perfectly illustrate the fundamental principles of our economic system. Where there is a demand for high quality goods or experiences and in-depth, expert knowledge, there is clearly a desire to offer the best version of just about anything. How wonderful that, in some cases, just a spoonful of meltingly smooth nut butter can be the answer.

Third Man Records (below) welcomes its customers to a quirky and rarefied universe dedicated to vinyl, sold here like black gold. Deyrolle (right) has made an international name for itself as a specialist in animal taxidermy.

MARIN MONTAGUT

Curiosities
Paris, France
Opened 2020

One of the many secrets of the magical Jardin du Luxembourg is a store door that takes you straight to the Paris of the 1900s. Bienvenue chez Marin Montagut. A qualified illustrator, Montagut chose a former upholstery store, gave his name to it, and transformed it into a jewel from another era.

Marin Montagut's miscellany ranges from decorative display cases and botanical prints to delicate glassware and porcelain. Treasures such as the popular **vitrines à merveilles** and **livres à secrets**, the elegant silk scarves, and the filigree plaster sculptures are all created by hand in the Paris studio; every one of his creations are made in Paris. For the store's design, Marin Montagut drew inspiration from old Parisian drugstores and the thousands of odds and ends they had for every budget. Old wooden floorboards creak in the first room as you browse through the displays and shelves. Historic wallpaper and heavy apothecary cabinets provide the poetic backdrop for this small, warm bubble of nostalgia. You return to the present enchanted—holding a souvenir from a Paris of bygone days.

MARIN MONTAGUT
SOUVENIRS DE PARIS FAITS À LA MAIN
MARIN MONTAGUT

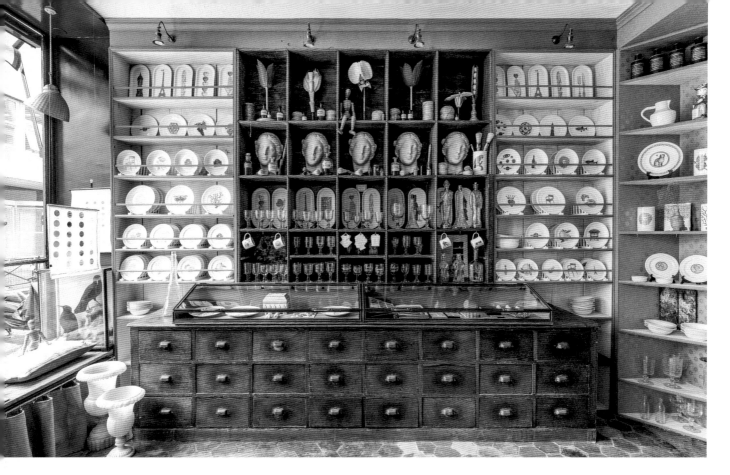

Among Marin Montagut's pretty treasures are the handmade and hand-painted Vitrines À Merveilles. You can see them on a shelf on the facing page. The small "Windows of Wonders" might include a papier-mâché open hand holding a heart, a cat, or a chair from the Jardin du Luxembourg. Marin Montagut designs and displays these wonders in glass-paneled frames.

À LA MÈRE DE FAMILLE

Chocolate
Paris, France
Opened in 1761

The tantalizing aroma of chocolate has wafted down the Rue du Faubourg, Montmartre, for more than 250 years. À la Mère de Famille, located at number 35 and painted in a deep green, is a Parisian institution. The Dolfi family took over the French capital's oldest chocolate store at the turn of the millennium and now looks after its heritage with care and sensitivity. Patterned tiles, dark wood shelving, and peg-shaped pendant lights hark back to the golden age of the late 19th century. The popular confections, spreads, candies, fruit pastes, and macarons are appetizingly presented in hand-labeled jars, drawers, and boxes. They are made in the company's very own workshop, two hours south of Paris, where new delicacies are constantly being added to the historical recipes. The original store has also grown. Today, 15 branches of À la Mère de Famille "sweeten" the inner Parisian arrondissements with historic façades and characteristic lettering—a true feast for the eyes.

ASTIER DE VILLATTE

Ceramics
Paris, France
Opened in 1996

In the early 1990s, together with a few friends and family members, Ivan Pericoli and Benoît Astier de Villatte designed their first dinnerware collections. They had met while studying at the École des Beaux-Arts in Paris and shared the same enthusiasm for still life, tableware, and anything "exquisite." The launch of their first store on Rue Saint-Honoré, one of the oldest streets in the French capital, was a resounding success. Parisian customers love the growing assortment of tableware and ceramic objects. Over the years, they have added furniture, scented candles, **eaux de cologne**, Christmas ornaments, stationery, and lighting.

The two enterprising business partners established the second store, shown here, on the Left Bank in 2016. Around the same time, they rescued one of the world's last hot-metal-type printers and published their first book, **Ma vie à Paris**, in their own publishing house. In 2021, Astier de Villatte made sure the partnership's 25th anniversary was commemorated with a fitting milestone: the partners opened their first store outside Paris, in Seoul.

When the company was founded in 1996, Astier de Villatte unveiled its first plates at the Maison & Objet in Paris. Dealers from all over the world quickly demanded more—at first, to no avail. It was only when **Star Wars** director George Lucas personally asked for matching cups for his new plates that the founders relented and designed the first cups three years later.

The cups were followed by teapots, sugar bowls, and decorative
pieces that were not necessarily practical, but certainly distinctive
and beautiful. Today, the label employs around 70 artists.

DEYROLLE
DEYROLLE

DEYROLLE

LE PRINCE JARDINIER

DEYROLLE

Taxidermy
Paris, France
Opened in 1831

Isn't it extraordinary? Deyrolle now works with UNESCO and was an official partner of the 2015 Paris Climate Change Conference! Founder Jean-Baptiste Deyrolle would have approved of this development. Deyrolle opened his eponymous store in the early 19th century when he was a taxidermist at the city's natural history museum. He wanted to introduce his visitors to the world's wild beauty, explain its finely woven connections to them, and persuade them to be part of active nature conservation. Today, his concerns are more relevant than ever.

In the winding rooms of this world-famous Paris institution, lions and cheetahs roam and peer at giraffes and zebras. Bats, flamingoes, and fossils coexist harmoniously. Nature's infinite and fantastic richness is assembled here in just a few square yards, turning the historic taxidermy shop into an overflowing museum. Yet Deyrolle seems to manage to keep up with the times and pursue its mission. As recently as 2007, Deyrolle's legendary illustrated plates were published as a book called **Deyrolle pour l'Avenir**—that is, "Deyrolle for the Future."

Ammonites, fossilized sea urchins, and precious stones such as amethysts are among the many items stored in Deyrolle's wooden display cases. Corals and giant clams glisten between carefully preserved birds in the room next door.

Deyrolle owes its current existence primarily to the support of fans from all over France. When a fire in 2008 destroyed the original store, a massive wave of solidarity quickly extinguished the last embers. Among the many donors was the fashion label Hermès, which promptly relaunched its popular **Plumes** ("Feathers") scarf design and donated all proceeds to Deyrolle.

DOLCE & GABBANA

Fashion
Rome, Italy
Opened in 2019

When it comes to the Italian fashion label Dolce & Gabbana, everybody knows that more is more! Paris-based architecture firm Carbondale has successfully translated this mantra into a dazzling store interior. The impressive size of the boutique is an optical illusion created using baroque techniques. From the entrance, the room size, ceiling height, column dimensions, and floor patterns decrease proportionally to achieve the required illusion of depth. The Murano glass chandeliers heighten the effect: they were designed in three different sizes, especially for the store.

The stunning centerpiece, however, is the Digital Gallery, which catapults Baroque Rome into the future. A continuous mirror wall visually transforms the semi-arched boutique area into a dome. Spanning it—digitally—is a beautiful fresco by Austrian Baroque painter Paul Troger. Curved LED screens completely cover the wall and ceiling, showing Hercules and Athena enveloped by dark clouds, thunder, and lightning that slowly give way to the rising sun.

Designers used 15 different types of marble, streaked with bright yellow and red or light-blue quartz, among many other variations. Traditional Italian craftsmanship techniques were used to create this phenomenal stone floor.

Cosmetics and
accessories
Paris, France
Opened in 2014

During the complicated negotiations for the small store on Rue Bonaparte, it transpired that the grandfather of prospective buyer Victoire de Taillac-Touhami had saved the owners of the original from Nazi persecution. The deal was quickly sealed. In 2014, Victoire and her husband, Ramdane Touhami, revived the Officine Universelle Buly cosmetics brand, founded at the beginning of the 19th century.

For the brand's first store, the French-Moroccan creative director envisioned a store utterly faithful to the original style of Buly's historic apothecaries—no extravagance was off limits. The impressive wooden cabinets are handmade and decorated with ornamentation in the Louis XV style. Here, old apothecary jars of all shapes and sizes exude historical flair. The lacquered floor tiles were fired at a low temperature in 5,000-year-old Etruscan kilns in Umbria, Italy. The process results in individual color nuances and the intended patina: today, the tiles look as if countless customers have been walking on them since the 19th century.

No extravagance is taboo for Creative Director Ramdane Touhami. For this interior, he chose, among other things, a mother-of-pearl faucet from a chateau in the Loire Valley, the finest ornaments even for the radiators, and precious Brèche de Bénou marble to adorn the counter's display surfaces. Brèche de Bénou is also found in the palace of Versailles, the Louvre, and the Opéra Garnier.

OFFICINE UNIVERSELLE BULY

Cosmetics and accessories
Tokyo, Japan
Opened in 2017

This second branch in Tokyo is even more sensational than Officine Universelle Buly's first store,
located in Paris (p.156). At first glance, it's hard
to see that the two halves of the Tokyo shop combine to make up one space. The historical side
of the store, to the right, represents the heritage cosmetics brand, founded in 1803 and relaunched over 200 years later by entrepreneurial
couple Victoire de Taillac-Touhami and Ramdane
Touhami. The counter, shelves, and ceiling are
made of warm walnut wood, referencing the
Parisian pharmacies that sold the label's first
powders, oils, and cosmetics in the 19th century.

In contrast, the newer half of the store
(to the left) is symbolic of the present and future. Japan's most modern side is on display here.
Beneath the glossy stretch ceiling, polished concrete forms a wall of small half-arches in which
select herbs and medicinal plants encased in
resin are displayed. The dividing line between
the two store areas is painted in gold, following
the traditional Japanese practice of **kintsugi**, or
"golden joinery."

On the right, turned wooden columns, refined paneled ceilings, and carved lion heads; on the left, polished concrete and cool, light, transparent resin. The contrast between the two areas could not be starker. However, the half-arches and warm turquoise create a unifying effect here.

VOLGARE

Fashion
Milan, Italy
Opened in 2022

Volgare's range is just as offbeat as its mix of colors, textures, and patterns. The Milan store sells select fashion items and accessories for men, and pairs them with stylish motorcycle helmets. For the eclectic vibe, the store's motorcycle-loving owner enlisted designer Gema Gutiérrez of the Spanish studio Puntofilipino. She has blended Moroccan, Mexican, Spanish, and Portuguese traditions to create an exuberant interior.

The classy base is Turkish terrazzo flooring, contrasting with the purple wall tiles by Italian design firm Studiopepe and the colorful blocks of stripes, round mirrors, and soft drapes. The lustrous glass bricks by the Spanish label Vitroland effectively set off the shoes and garments. The exciting color palette, from turquoise to amber, reflects the city of Milan's creative side. Soft armchairs and polished wood side tables invite you to relax with friends. With so much design horsepower, you wouldn't want to be without your motorcycle helmet.

This multi-faceted interior has been chosen for the 2023 Gold German Design Award. According to the jury, the space is "by no means arbitrary, but rather a coherent concept in its entirety." Congratulations!

SABAH HOUSE NEW YORK

Shoes
New York, New York, USA
Opened in 2022

With its soft cushions and thick rugs, Sabah House New York evokes the caravanserais along the ancient Silk Road. The store for hand-sewn Turkish leather shoes is more living room than classic retail store. No wonder customers like to linger here and often return as friends. Interestingly, charismatic owner Mickey Ashmore never intended to become a shoe retailer.

When he went to Turkey to find a replacement for his favorite shoes that had worn out, he met the oldest family of shoemakers in the country. The shoes known as Sabahs take their name from the Turkish word for morning. Today, Mickey has his Sabahs handmade with the best leather in Turkey—simultaneously helping to safeguard an artisan craft threatened with extinction. He designed his New York store with the help of architect Ishtiaq Jabir Rafiuddin. When Mickey joins his customers for tea at the store's bar, Sabah House becomes a modern caravanserai, where Turkish culture, commerce, and community are happily at home.

After selling his first handmade shoes at parties in his apartment, Mickey Ashmore opened several Sabah Houses in the USA and one in London. In Amagansett, Austin, Dallas, and San Francisco, Sabahs in all colors fill the shelves. Thanks to a unique tanning process, the leather ages beautifully and develops a dignified patina over time.

ALICE THROUGH THE LOOKING GLASS

Books and accessories
London, U.K.
Opened in 2012

In some stores, you can lose yourself miraculously, like Alice in Wonderland. In their magical store called Alice Through The Looking Glass, Jake Fior and Jo Humphris sell rare, unusual, and classic editions of books inspired by British author Lewis Carroll's well-loved tale and its sequel, which gives the store its name. Art prints, stationery, ceramics, and accessories complete the self-contained universe. Many unusual (and unsalable) finds have turned the store into a museum. Major institutions ask the store for loans of its precious objects (for example the Victoria & Albert Museum in 2022).

For the interior, Jake and Jo eschewed the help of an interior designer and created their own unique aesthetic. The chandelier is from a hotel ballroom and once sparkled above a dancing Frank Sinatra. The oversized mirror is also one-of-a-kind. Jake and Jo have combined antique cabinets and mood lighting with silver-colored walls. But the interior is constantly changing thanks to new finds—much like the story's Wonderland.

MINTCHI

Croissants
São Paulo, Brazil
Opened in 2019

Mintchi's architecture is as crisp and light as its delicious croissants. Founder Luisa Garbarino came up with the design in collaboration with São Paulo-based Dezembro Arquitetos. They constructed the small store—a former ten-by-sixteen-foot garage—in several layers, rather like a perfect croissant. The airy first layer consists of upright bricks with cement-filled holes. Fun fact: The construction workers got creative, too, and used an improvised spray nozzle to complete the work.

Floating feather-light above Mintchi's inviting bench and sales counter is the ceiling, covered in hanging cardboard tubes. Some tubes serve as light fixtures, bathing the store in a golden, croissant-colored light. Gleaming brass details above the checkout area enhance this effect. The back of the store is separated by a glass window that offers a view of Mintchi's beautiful bakery. No wonder Luisa's customers prefer to savor their oven-warm croissants on the spot.

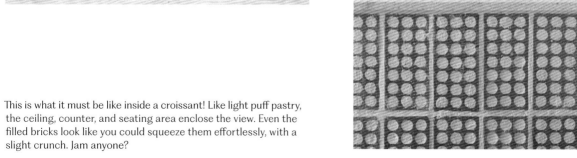

This is what it must be like inside a croissant! Like light puff pastry, the ceiling, counter, and seating area enclose the view. Even the filled bricks look like you could squeeze them effortlessly, with a slight crunch. Jam anyone?

COALBROOK

Bathroom essentials
London, U.K.
Opened in 2022

Coalbrook, a young brand creating luxury bathroom fixtures, found the perfect home in a monumental industrial building in the London borough of Clerkenwell. Local interior architects Holloway Li converted a former factory from the early 1900s into an experiential showroom, including a co-working space. Traditional craftsmanship, history, and modernity literally flow into one another here.

Shower heads, faucets, and waterfall fixtures invite you to try them out. Water rushes or splashes into the refined sinks, tubs, and drains. Coalbrook's basement reveals itself as a mystical engine room. The dark, bronze-colored industrial boilers are the perfect backdrop for the gleaming fixtures. A massive stone staircase leads to the bright first floor. Here, the industrial theme is broken up by orange- and amber-colored panels made of synthetic resin, which serve as modern display units for shower heads and faucets. The Victorian appearance of the panels, in turn, references the brand's roots and the era of the Industrial Revolution.

Coalbrook's products are showcased in the building's basement and first floor, where several co-working spaces, a conference room, and a bar complement the showrooms. Depending on the time of day, you'll see architects and designers meeting their clients here.

Among the most striking interior details are the colored panels (above and right). The transparent resin, which appears almost liquid, contrasts in materiality with the panels' decorative cornices, moldings, tiles, and half-arches, subverting their traditional Victorian form.

KORA BAKERY

Bakery products
Athens, Greece
Opened in 2020

When Maria Alafouzou and Ianthi Michalaki opened Kora Bakery in the middle of the COVID-19 pandemic, they asked Athens-based en-route architecture to swiftly integrate the mandatory social distancing rules into the interior design. The transparent shelves that hold the crisp delicacies can be opened and closed from the customer's or vendor's side, making them ideal for minimizing direct contact. Plenty of visibility makes up for the lack of interaction, and today it's a stylish remnant of the challenging times.

Maria and Ianthi conjure up high-quality sourdough bread, cakes, sweets, and beautiful viennoiseries that are well-known far beyond the borders of their Athens neighborhood. Small details have also made the Kora Bakery a modern community place: a small water tap to the left of the entrance, for example, is reminiscent of the traditional **vrisi**, a public, central water point in Greek villages. Like in the countryside, Athenians can help themselves to water here day and night. Bread and water are simultaneously the most basic and precious things, are they not?

The designers created Kora's unusually elevated and recessed terrace area as a chic stage for their baked goods. Rotating metal shelves provide transparent views from the sales area to the bakery, visually connected by the square tiles and yellow ceiling.

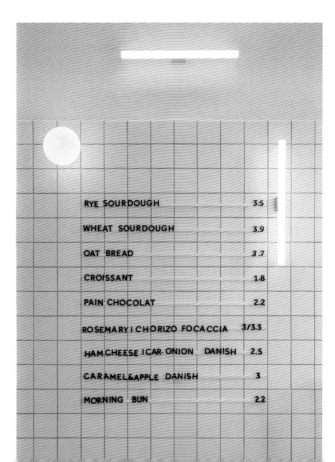

RYE SOURDOUGH 3.5

WHEAT SOURDOUGH 3.9

OAT BREAD 3.7

CROISSANT 1.8

PAIN CHOCOLAT 2.2

ROSEMARY I CHORIZO FOCACCIA 3/3.3

HAM·CHEESE I CAR· ONION DANISH 2.5

CARAMEL&APPLE DANISH 3

MORNING BUN 2.2

THIRD MAN RECORDS

Vinyl records and more
London, U.K.
Opened in 2021

As if by the laws of nature, Nashville, Tennessee seems to export one thing above all: outstanding entertainment. After a first store in Nashville and a second in Detroit, U.S. musician Jack White of White Stripes fame opened Third Man Records' third store in London's historic Soho district. Vinyl is almost incidental here—the bright yellow store is full of surprises. For example, its Blue Basement hosts more or less underground concerts for up to 60 guests.

There's more: Jack had a recording booth from the 1950s flown in specially from Nashville. Here, musicians and interested customers can record their own songs directly onto vinyl. The "Literarium" on the first floor—an invention by Canadian artist Craig Small—ejects small books when you insert a coin. The record shelves are stocked with classics and limited-edition collectibles. But behind this store and all the entertainment, Third Man Records is, in fact, primarily a record label, and it's breaking into the European market.

Third Man Records is a playground for musicians and anyone aspiring to be one. In addition to its 1950s flair, the popular recording booth, and personal memorabilia, visitors will find merch from the label, which also uses the store as a drop-in center for musicians under contract.

If you pick up the phone in the phone booth, you can hear recordings by Jack White, the founder of Third Man Records. There are personal reasons behind the choice of London for Third Man's European location: It was here that the White Stripes celebrated their first great successes with hits like "Seven Nation Army."

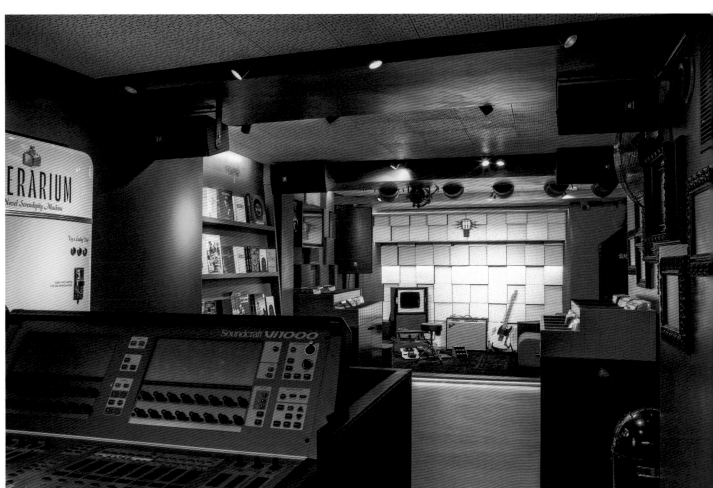

SUPERETTE ANNEX

Cannabis products
Toronto, Canada
Opened in 2022

What looks like an Italian deli actually sells something a little bit different: Superette's shelves are filled with cannabis products, ranging from pre-rolled joints and various types of marijuana to accessories such as bongs, rolling papers, ashtrays, and lighters. To match its green-striped awning, the company's in-house design team combined pale green shelving, cannabis-themed prints, and inviting highboards. Bar chairs, lamps, and Superette's logo add red accents.

With two urban university campuses just a few blocks away, Superette Annex, the Canadian label's seventh store, has its biggest target audience nearby. Admission to the store is permitted only if you are 19 or older. So the students can enjoy the interior, buy and smoke cannabis, and also use the store to co-work, study together, and go on relaxed dates. When hunger strikes, the red Munchie Phone on the wall can be used to order directly from the Jewish deli next door. Is it an illusion, or did the green of the checkerboard floor somehow get more vivid just now?

The founders of Superette want, in their words, to "make buying cannabis as enjoyable as consuming it." To set themselves apart from other cannabis stores, they deliberately chose a fresh approach, combining unexpected design with a familiar retail environment. Thoughtful details, from the splash of red paint to the Munchie Phone, ensure a high entertainment factor.

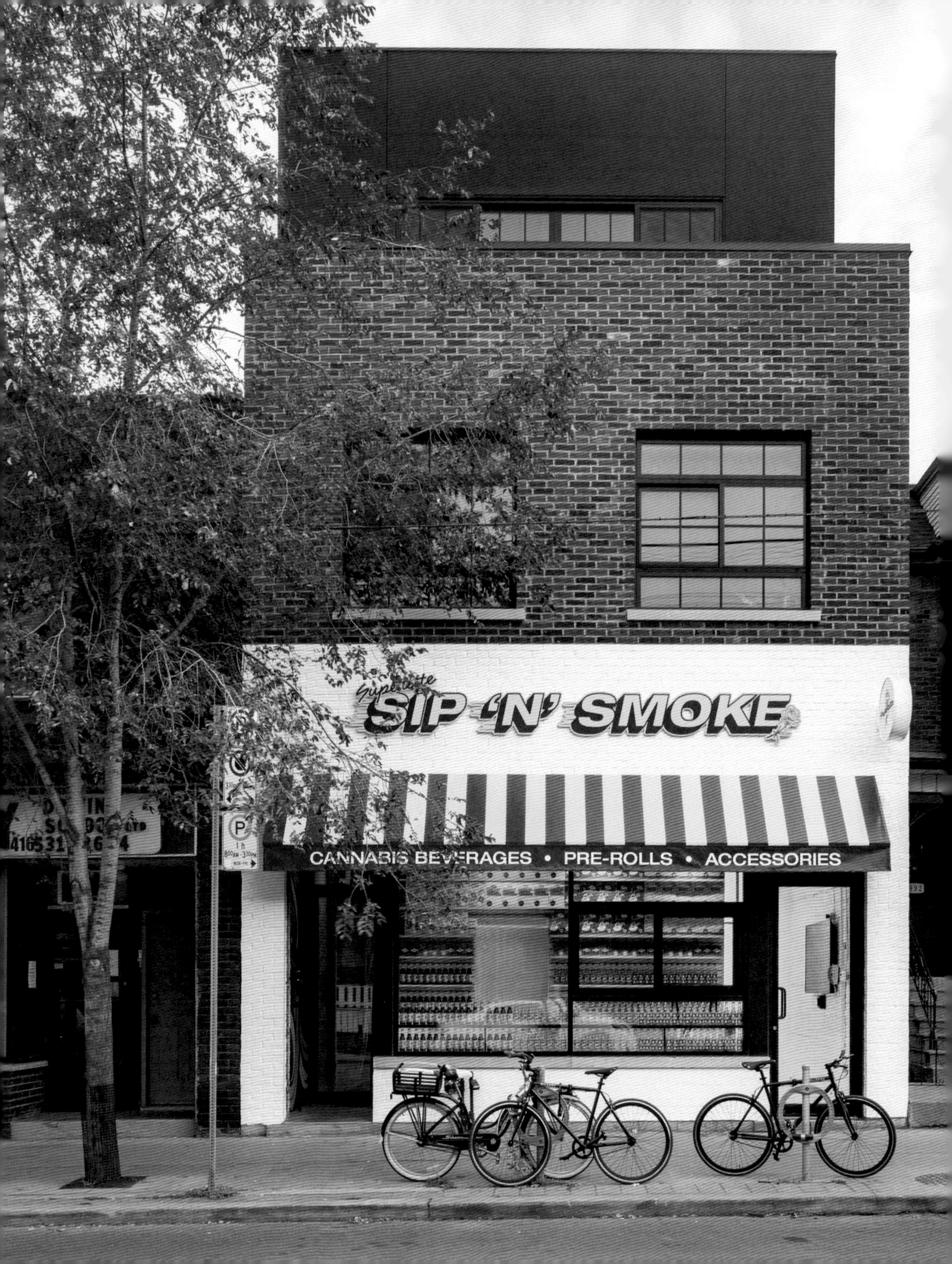
SIP 'N' SMOKE
CANNABIS BEVERAGES • PRE-ROLLS • ACCESSORIES

SIP 'N' SMOKE

Cannabis products
Toronto, Canada
Opened in 2021

Like the Canadian brand's other store, Superette (p. 198), the Trinity-Bellwoods neighborhood location turns cannabis shopping into a hyperlocal experience. Sip 'n' Smoke sells pre-rolled joints and cannabis-infused drinks specifically for a picnic in the leafy green space next door, at Trinity Bellwoods Park. Like in a self-service cafeteria, customers take a tray and fill it up with their favorite products. Additionally, the store sells practical accessories for the park, such as picnic blankets, portable speakers, and bottle openers.

Mimi Lam and Drummond Munro, Superette's founders, take a local approach to an immersive concept that has been integrated harmoniously into its neighborhood from the start. The team draws inspiration from local retailers' interiors for all Superette stores. The design of each store is based on familiar surroundings—from a corner store, candy store, florist, or (as here) a cafeteria. All the stores combine comforting nostalgia with contemporary cannabis products.

Humor is also a top priority at Sip 'n' Smoke. Customers can order from a
partner restaurant via a permanently installed telephone and get advice
on the range of cannabis products from a "budtender." Quirky ideas like
this make all of Superette's stores popular destinations.

Firing on all Channels, Real and Digital

In today's world of metaverse, social media, and augmented reality, there is every reason to combine online with offline.

See "Discover" designer Michel Ducaroy's iconic Togo sofa on Instagram and buy it via direct messaging or email, and then pick it up at the store in the evening—Home Union in Brooklyn makes it possible. The store for vintage furniture belongs to a growing breed of stores accessible to customers through every conceivable channel. The boundaries between online and offline have been blurred to create a seamless shopping experience.

The trend is substantiated by the numbers. Market research institutes have discovered that omnichannel customers—i.e., customers who use several channels to shop at the same store—are almost twice as likely as single-channel customers to make purchases. Accordingly, they also spend much more money. If a customer comes into a store having visited the associated website in the previous 24 hours, the likelihood of them making a purchase increases by up to three times. Meanwhile, according to market research by the consultancy Accenture, 77% of Generation Z prefer physical stores to online stores. Brick-and-mortar retailing is still irreplaceable—but in a different way and with a digital sidekick.

Big brands are leading the way. They deliberately use digital functionality to create immersive experiences and provide customers with practical decision-making aids. Augmented reality is particularly popular. The furniture store IKEA, for example, has developed an app that allows customers to view various pieces of furniture digitally in their own homes. With a click, a table switches from glass to wood, from low to high, and from A to B. Car brands such as Audi also offer realistic visualizations of the colors, materials, and features of the car of your dreams.

It's a win-win situation—customers who know exactly what they want make much more targeted and faster purchases. Merchant (p. 42) in Los Angeles has demonstrated that immersive experiences also work offline. Instead of an AR app, the interior store has furnished an entire vacation home with couches, curtains, and accessories. Patrons can test out the whole range, feel the materials, fall in love with the products, and buy them in-store after their vacation. This is where the sphere of influence of digital reality ends. We cannot (as of yet) digitally reproduce the experiences of touch or smell, although visuals and sounds can be replicated and enhanced. If you let your imagination run wild and combine both realities meaningfully, surprising possibilities open up. In Toronto, the Canada Goose store has created a super-realistic world of customer experience. In the store's own Cold Room, customers can try out boots and down jackets at -25 °C (-13 °F), with

"Studies on Generation Z have shown that brick-and-mortar retailing is still irreplaceable—but in a different way and with a digital sidekick."

Home Union (p. 206) and Spazio Permano (p. 207) initially existed only as online stores. Henne (above) relies on a harmonious in-store and online design. You could say Mango Teen (left) offers a sneak peek into a possible future scenario.

snowy ambience and simulated black ice included. Interestingly, the Canada Goose store only serves as a service-oriented experience area: Once you choose a pair of gloves or a jacket on-site, you don't take them with you right away, as you would usually, but have them delivered to your home the same evening.

It isn't just that the concept of retail can be expanded. It has to be. The young, in particular, are growing up with a new understanding of the digital world, meeting online to play games and taking advantage of digital learning opportunities. Much like in the days of the great explorers, today, the undreamt-of possibilities of virtual worlds are being explored by mostly young adventurers. Anyone who wants to win and keep customers in this climate is well advised to sail along with them.

In Barcelona, Mango Teen has taken the digital metaverse as its style model and created a futuristic boutique for teenagers. Based on focus groups with 11-to-13-year-olds, award-winning design firm Masquespacio developed an otherworldly interior modeled on a new reality. Mango Teen is a digital world you can touch and a metaverse you can walk into with fashion to try on. It has perfect social media backdrops, bright colors, and a thousand analog and virtual corners to explore. It also offers "click-and-collect" so you can pick up your favorite items ordered online. Teenagers—the customers of tomorrow—love it.

IMAGES D'ORIENT

Ceramics
Beirut, Lebanon
Opened in 2019

Images d'Orient's warmly patterned assortment promises a piece of Lebanon for everyone. Siblings Peggy and Charbel Raphaël founded their brand in 2000 to preserve part of their homeland's cultural heritage. The plan to fuse traditional patterns and myths with affordable everyday objects paid off: today, their dinnerware sets, vases, tiles, and accessories are sold in over 50 countries.

The store in Ashrafieh, one of Beirut's oldest neighborhoods, is both boutique and showroom. Lebanese studio Rabih Geha Architects (RG/A) designed the interior in keeping with the brand's modern Middle Eastern aesthetic. Contemporary elements like perforated steel and modular light fixtures contrast with rich colors and warm terrazzo. Arched shelving showcases bestsellers like the Birds of Paradise ceramic series, which figuratively explores classical poetry and medieval myths. Other series feature traditional patterns and modern interpretations of tales from the heritage of past civilizations—cultural treasures for every day.

Gray Aggloceppo terrazzo floors, crisp white walls, blue round arches, and the bright red ceiling give the store its modern Mediterranean feel. Aluminum shelving and modular light fixtures add a dash of futurism— a real statement in Ashrafieh, one of Beirut's oldest neighborhoods.

O'FLOWER

Flowers
Hwaseong, South Korea
Opened in 2022

Somewhere between a laboratory and a space shuttle—that's the aesthetic of o'flower, online florist Okkot's first store. Seoul-based architecture firm Plainoddity designed the interior as an unobtrusive backdrop to showcase the floral splendor on offer. The sizeable triangular metal counter, whose shape is echoed by the sky-light, is set against a fresh, sky-blue backdrop. Next to it, astonishingly, is a large table with eight chairs. What is that doing at a florist?

      The table is the centerpiece of the concept of o'flower. A bouquet of flowers is one of the most personal gifts you can give someone. The idea is that if you help to create the bouquet, the gift becomes even more personal. The table becomes an experimental laboratory where customers can compose their own bouquets. The ingredients for the floral experiment are displayed in glass containers mounted around the sales area. All around the table are conical lab flasks ready for you to use—they make excellent vases and also match with the store's décor.

The angular stainless steel furniture and the functional
lights turn the store into a laboratory. Customers become
researchers, experimenting with flower combinations and
their own sense of aesthetics.

By allowing its customers to participate actively in the bouquets' design, o'flower is part of a growing trend towards ensuring strong customer loyalty through event-like personalization. Choosing and arranging the flowers becomes the highlight, letting customers find creative expression.

Delicatessen
Granada, Spain
Opened in 2021

Altelier's delicious oils, cheeses, and fine wines are displayed like works of art. Working with the Spanish graphic design agency Buenaventura, Gema Gutiérrez, CEO of the Spanish interior-design studio Puntofilipino, chose a sleek aesthetic for the design, showing off the products on offer rather than competing with them. The basis of the store's design in the main space is the hand-finished, light-gray resin floor. Above it, pale yellow, coral, and washed-out turquoise add muted color accents. The white tiles create a kitchen-like feel, and the display counters resemble kitchen islands. The materials used are mostly locally sourced.

In the basement, select wines are stored in a modern wine cellar with terrazzo flooring, and historic jugs trace the arc of history. Upstairs, whole cured hams hang on the wall like an installation. Recessed spotlights and designer lighting set the scene for the culinary delights. In Altelier, delicatessen shopping becomes a gallery visit. And rightly so: after all, isn't good food the noblest of all arts?

The designers have covered some walls with unpigmented lime as a warm contrast to the uniformly square tiles. Natural stone, tiles, resin, and lacquer complete the palette of materials.

Focusing on a few high-quality ingredients is good, and not just in food. The designers have applied this idea to the interior, spotlighting spices, wine, and more.

LUPH

Fashion
Huế, Vietnam
Opened in 2021

Fashion design label Luph commissioned the Vietnamese architects Limdim House Studio to design a geometric store made of concrete, glass, and metal. The unusual façade arouses the curiosity of passersby while maintaining privacy inside. Warm daylight falls on the elegant collections through large windows and the triangular courtyard at the store's heart. These design ideas simultaneously open up the space and link the building with its surroundings.

A gallery adds several square yards to the small store and provides different viewing angles. The first set of stairs flows seamlessly to the reception counter. Upstairs, a round door creates a visual counterbalance to the block-like character of the store. The architects developed a finely tuned spotlight and downlight system that showcases the clothing displays. LEDs installed at floor level accentuate the store's attractive corners and edges. And since light is inevitably a design feature itself, the glass cloud lamps also serve as a popular photo motif for design fans.

The triangular inner courtyard (right) contrasts Luph's massive block elements with a delicate lightness. In addition, the glazed mezzanine, which almost seems to float, breaks the heavy character of the concrete and thus highlights an entirely new side of the material.

AXEL ARIGATO

Fashion
Copenhagen, Denmark
Opened in 2019

Albin Johansson believes that the future of retail lies in a strong sense of community for the customer. For the co-founder of Swedish fashion label Axel Arigato, the Copenhagen store embodies the brand's soul. His co-founder, Max Svardh, designs all the stores in collaboration with Stockholm-based studio Christian Halleröd. The stores share design features, yet they are individual, inviting, unusual, and memorable.

The Axel Arigato store in Copenhagen plays with the surprising contrast of its traditionally historic façade and a brutalist-minimalist interior. A monumental concrete staircase connects the two floors and serves as a display for sneakers, fashion, and art. The neon, futuristic, cloud-like installation pedestals are eye-catching. They are both shelves and works of art in their own right. Floor-to-ceiling mirrors reinforce the effect of a parallel world. There is also plenty of room for imagination. With weekly events, Axel Arigato delivers on its promise to be an active part of a growing community.

AXEL ARIGATO

Max Svardh approaches the interiors of his stores like he does sneaker design. According to Axel Arigato's creative director, "The shape of the object comes first, the material is secondary." The sculptural shelves were handmade from jesmonite and covered with neon and metallic high-gloss lacquer. Do you think Jeff Koons even likes wearing sneakers?

SORGENFRI

Concept store
Oslo, Norway
Opened in 2019

Is it a store, an art gallery, a café, or an event space? Somehow, Sorgenfri is a bit of everything. A hybrid riposte to the luxury boutiques in downtown Oslo, Creative Director Ingrid Bredholt's project explicitly supports local and Scandinavian artists, creatives, and workshops. Sorgenfri's select collections range from music, crafts, and books to jewelry, furniture, and accessories. The sustainable streetwear on offer is intended as a statement against fast fashion. The store doubles as a sensational gallery space for ever-changing art exhibitions.

On the first floor, raw concrete contrasts with gleaming metal and pink marble, which is also used for the bar. Ingrid also runs her own coffee shop and a natural wine bar with vegetarian bar food, which can also be enjoyed on the 80-square-meter (860-square-foot) sun terrace in summer. Sorgenfri's secret highlight, however, is the basement. Here, roughly hewn caves transport visitors into an eclectic parallel world created—how else—by local artisans.

It's hard to imagine that this store is located in a registered historic building from the late 19th century. Its interior is an intentional counter-design to the classic lines of the building and was created through the owner's collaboration with a local artists' collective.

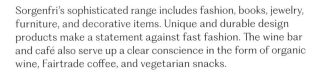

Sorgenfri's sophisticated range includes fashion, books, jewelry, furniture, and decorative items. Unique and durable design products make a statement against fast fashion. The wine bar and café also serve up a clear conscience in the form of organic wine, Fairtrade coffee, and vegetarian snacks.

DOVER STREET MARKET LOS ANGELES

Concept store
Los Angeles, California, USA
Opened in 2018

Dover Street Market Los Angeles—DSMLA for short—is the sixth store of the famous brand, following branches in London, Beijing, Singapore, New York, and Tokyo. In a 1,400-square-meter (15,000-square-foot) space, DSMLA reimagines the concept store with its self-proclaimed motto of "beautiful chaos." Japanese founder Rei Kawakubo founded the fashion label Comme des Garçons back in 1969 and runs the enterprise with her husband, Adrian Joffe. The couple shares a vision of a creative hub for art, culture, and luxury retail.

Shops-in-shops like Gucci sell hard-to-find special editions. In between, you'll find select fashion from It-labels like Raf Simons, Simone Rocha, and Maison Margiela. Kawakubo also likes to curate up-and-coming labels, giving them the chance to grow here in lab conditions. Numerous local artists have contributed to the store's installations. And if you want to chill out for a while, there's the Rose Bakery, where you can enjoy a coffee in the California sun.

At DSMLA, entire design universes and everyday art collide. Here, visitors can experience creativity in real time. The fact that the exhibitors' visions outpace each other is intentional: Inspiration plus a little pressure naturally leads to peak performance.

The concept of the Dover Street Market is as radical as its look.
Twice a year, the legendary "New Beginning" takes place here
in January and July. All partner labels completely dismantle their
areas, only to rise from the ashes two days later with a new
interior design and product range.

THINK
BIG—
SHOP
SMALL

Unique Stores
and Contemporary
Retail Design

This book was conceived, edited, and designed by gestalten.

Edited by Robert Klanten
Contributing Editor: Marianne Julia Strauss
Editorial Support: Effie Efthymiadi

Texts by Marianne Julia Strauss

Translation from German to English by Laila Friese
with First Edition Translations Ltd, Cambridge, U.K.
Editorial Management by Lars Pietzschmann

Cover, design and layout by Stefan Morgner

Photo editor: Madeline Dudley-Yates

Typeface: Fragment by Francesca Bolognini and Mat Desjardins

Cover image by Polina Parcevskya/Courtesy of PUNTOFILIPINO

Printed by Grafisches Centrum Cuno GmbH & Co. KG, Calbe (Saale)
Made in Germany

Published by gestalten, Berlin 2023
ISBN 978-3-96704-094-4

© Die Gestalten Verlag GmbH & Co. KG, Berlin 2023

For more information, and to order books, please visit www.gestalten.com

Bibliographic information published by the Deutsche Nationalbibliothek.
The Deutsche Nationalbibliothek lists this publication in the Deutsche
Nationalbibliografie; detailed bibliographic data is available online at
www.dnb.de

None of the content in this book was published in exchange for payment
by commercial parties or designers; gestalten selected all included work
based solely on its artistic merit.

This book was printed on paper certified according to the standards of the FSC®.